A is for ARUBA

A Family Alphabet Book

Written and Illustrated By

Lori Flying Fish

Copyright Laurie Ruhl, 2012

All rights reserved. Published by Create Space.

No part of this publication may be reproduced, stored in a retrieval system, transmitted in any form or by any means, electronic, mechanical, photocopying, recording, or otherwise without prior written permission of the publisher and author/illustrator.

Graphic design by Laurie Ruhl.

For in formation regarding permission,
Contact us at our website:
www.Create Space.com

ISBN: 978-1475283389

Library of Congress Number: 201290820

Printed in the U.S.A.

Printed May 2012

Dedication

To the letters from
A to Z
That form the words
To express my fondest memories
Of Mi Dushi Aruba

LIGNUM VITAE   LITTLE LAGOON

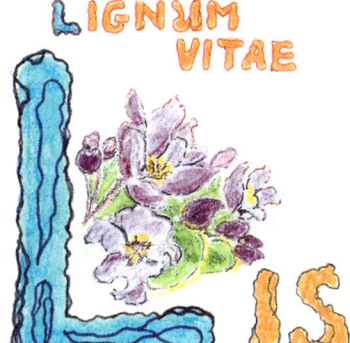

L IS FOR

LAGOONS

LONGTAIL BASS

SPANISH LAGOON

LANCER

DRAGONETTE

BIG LAGOON

N IS FOR

Natural Pool

Nasi Goreng

Homage to the

Night-Blooming Cereus

Natural Bridge

Pasa un Bon Dia   Papiamentu   Masha Danki

Na Bo Brisa Bon Nochi Te Aworo Mi Dushi Aruba

Bon Bini Bon Dia Te Aworo Con Ta Bai?

Draw Your Favorite Island Pictures Here

Draw Your Favorite Island Pictures Here

Acknowledgements

"I am grateful to all the people that have supported this project since its inception and I want to offer them my heartfelt thanks: To all my writing friends in the Pine Island Writers, The Kids Stuff Group, and the CC Writers, who encouraged me and watched over the process; To Lynne Kemper, for providing expert class instruction and experienced critiquing; To her husband, Ron Kemper, for providing patient technical assistance in preparing the digital files; To Judy Loose, who guided me in the mechanics of navigating the intricate PC programs to bring this book to life; To Ashley Wilson and Joanna Rivera, for their consistently careful printing of my Father's slides that were inspirational for many of the drawings; And to Paul Holmes, for reassuring me that I could master this process and for answering a multitude of questions until it all came together in a book."

Lori Flying Fish